DATE DUE

ANDREW JACKSON

OUR SEVENTH PRESIDENT

by Ann Graham Gaines

THE CHILD'S WORLD®

Published by The Child's World®
1980 Lookout Drive • Mankato, MN 56003-1705
800-599-READ • www.childsworld.com

Acknowledgments
The Child's World®: Mary Berendes, Publishing Director

The Creative Spark: Mary McGavic, Project Director and Page Production;
Shari Joffe, Editorial Director; Deborah Goodsite, Photo Research

The Design Lab: Kathleen Petelinsek, Design

Content Adviser: Marsha A. Mullin, Chief Curator/Vice-President of Museum
Services, The Hermitage, Hermitage, Tennessee

Photos
Cover: Collection of the New York Historical Society, USA/The Bridgeman Art
Library International

Interior: Alamy: 15, 18 and 38 (North Wind Picture Archives); The Bridgeman
Art Library: 14 (Library of Congress, Washington D.C., USA), 19 (Chicago
History Museum, USA), 25, 35 (Private Collection, Peter Newark American
Pictures); Corbis: 4, 26 (Bettmann); Getty Images: 36 (Library Of Congress);
The Granger Collection, New York: 7, 8, 10, 11, 12, 20, 24, 28 and 39, 32, 33,
37; The Hermitage (Home of Andrew Jackson, Nashville, Tennessee): 6, 21, 23,
34; Historic Hudson Valley: 17 and 38; iStockphoto: 44 (Tim Fan); North Wind
Picture Archives: 5; Photo Researchers: 30; U.S. Air Force photo: 45; White
House Historical Association: 29.

Library of Congress Cataloging-in-Publication Data
Gaines, Ann.
  Andrew Jackson / by Ann Graham Gaines.
      p. cm. — (Presidents of the U.S.A.)
  Includes bibliographical references and index.
  ISBN 978-1-60253-036-2 (library bound : alk. paper)
  1. Jackson, Andrew, 1767–1845—Juvenile literature. 2. Presidents—United
States—Biography—Juvenile literature. I. Title.
  E382.G239 2008
  973.5'6092—dc22
  [B]
                                        2007042607

Printed in the United States of America • Mankato, MN
June, 2012 • PA02139

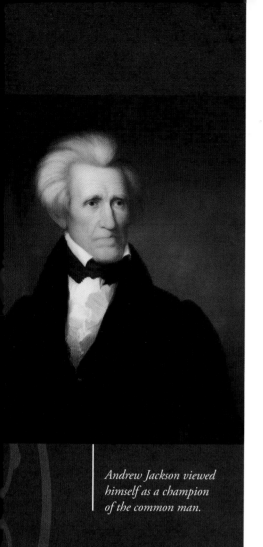

Andrew Jackson viewed himself as a champion of the common man.

TABLE OF CONTENTS

CHAPTER ONE

FRONTIER CHILDHOOD

Andrew Jackson, who became the seventh president of the United States in 1829, was different from the other presidents who came before him. He was the first president whose parents had been poor **immigrants.** He was also the first president elected from a **frontier** state. In office, he would distinguish himself in two ways. He protected the rights of those he considered "the people"— ordinary Americans who were not rich and did not hold a lot of power. On the other hand, he abused the rights of those he did not consider equal, especially Native Americans.

Andrew Jackson's parents came to the American **colonies** in 1765, just two years before their third son was born. They were poor people who came from Ireland to start a new life. Andrew's father was a farmer, also named

Andrew Jackson had a difficult childhood. Unlike the six presidents before him, he was born poor. By age 14, he had lost his entire family to war and illness.

Andrew Jackson. His mother's name was Elizabeth, but people called her Betty.

The Jacksons settled in a tiny region along the border of North Carolina and South Carolina called the Waxhaws. There they bought 200 acres of land. Before Andrew Jackson's father could plant crops, he had to clear the land. He had to chop down many trees to make way for his fields. One day early in the spring of 1767, he tried to move a heavy log. It was too big for him to move alone. He strained his heart and collapsed. By nighttime, he was dead.

Jackson was born in a simple cabin that may have looked much like this one. From his difficult childhood in South Carolina, he grew up to become a tough, courageous man known for his bad temper.

As a boy, Andrew Jackson was a wild redhead with lots of energy. He loved to ride horses and roughhouse. His family worried that he might hurt himself one day because he was so reckless.

The Jacksons already had two little boys: Hugh, who was four; and Robert, who was two. Just a few days after her husband died, Betty Jackson gave birth to Andrew, the future president. He was born on March 15, 1767.

As a child, Andrew was a tall, thin redhead who liked to run and jump. He loved to ride horses, too. Some children thought he was a bully. Adults complained about his temper, too.

Betty Jackson could not farm on her own, so she and her children moved in with relatives. She never had much money. Still, she paid for Andrew to go to a private school, because there was no public school in the Waxhaws.

By the time Andrew was five years old, he already knew how to read. He was always very smart. But even though he was good at math and reading, he could never be bothered to learn the rules of grammar or spelling.

The American **Revolution** began in 1775 in the northern colonies of New England. The people who lived in South Carolina knew all about the war. They read about it in newspapers and heard about it from visitors. Many people in South Carolina believed colonists were right to fight for freedom from England. They rejoiced when the Declaration of Independence was signed in 1776.

For a long time, the fighting took place far away from them. Even so, Andrew Jackson's brother Hugh

Although the American Revolution began in New England, battles were fought in the South as well. The Battle of Cowpens, shown here, took place in South Carolina. A force of 1,000 Americans won a huge victory against the British, eventually forcing them to withdraw from the area.

signed up and joined the American army. He died in battle in 1779.

In 1780, a British general named Charles Cornwallis sent soldiers into South Carolina. The British army needed supplies. He ordered his men to take items such as food and hay. Members of local **militias**—volunteer armies—gathered near the Waxhaws. They were preparing to fight the invaders. Suddenly, a huge force of British soldiers surprised them. About 100 of the **patriots,** including many of the Jacksons' friends and neighbors, died in the fighting that followed. Some patriots were shot in battle, but others gave up. They thought the British would make them prisoners of war.

After witnessing the Waxhaw Massacre (right), thirteen-year-old Andrew Jackson joined the American army to fight the British in the Revolutionary War.

When news of the battle reached the Jacksons, Betty took Robert and Andrew to the town's church, which was being used as a hospital. There they helped care for Americans who had been wounded in the battle.

The British soldiers killed the patriots they had captured. As a result, this battle became known as the Waxhaw Massacre. After it was over, the Jacksons and other residents of the area fled to North Carolina for a few weeks. When they returned home, Robert and Andrew were still furious about the British soldiers' treatment of their friends and neighbors. The brothers joined the American army. They were assigned to the **cavalry,** the part of the army that fought on horseback.

Robert was 16 years old. Many boys his age fought in the American Revolution. He was trained and went into battle. Andrew was just 13 years old. He was still too young to fight. Historians do not know exactly what he did in the army. He may have worked as a messenger or carried water to soldiers.

In April of 1781, both Jackson boys went home on leave. In South Carolina, they were captured by the British. One soldier ordered the boys to clean his boots. When they refused, he slashed them with his sword. Andrew and Robert were sent to a British prison camp in South Carolina. The conditions were terrible in the prison. Both boys were already wounded. Now they became sick with **smallpox.**

Betty Jackson traveled to the prison camp, hoping to help her sons. She went to see the commander in

When Andrew Jackson was 16, his grandfather in Ireland died. In his will, he left Andrew a great deal of money. Unfortunately, Andrew gambled the money away.

When Andrew Jackson was 14, he and his brother were taken prisoner by the British. When an officer ordered them to clean his boots, they bravely refused. As punishment, the British soldier cut the boys with his sword.

charge of the prison. She begged for the release of her sons and three other boys from the Waxhaws. The commander agreed to let the boys go free. Robert was so ill that he died just two days after they reached home. Betty Jackson nursed Andrew, and he recovered.

Toward the end of the war, Betty Jackson volunteered to go to Charleston, South Carolina. She worked as a nurse, helping injured and sick American soldiers.

The British allowed her on board prison ships. Within just a few weeks, she became sick with **cholera.** Andrew Jackson found out she had died when her belongings were sent back home. At age 14, he had lost his entire family. His father, mother, and two brothers had all died. He was all alone.

During the American Revolution, the British army kept some of its American prisoners on ships like this one, called the Jersey. *It was difficult to escape from these ships, and the conditions were terrible. A thousand men and boys were crammed into a small space. There was very little food. Lice and rats pestered the prisoners and spread disease. About 11,000 Americans died of disease and starvation on the* Jersey *during the Revolution.*

THE WEST

During the colonial era, Americans still lived in the eastern part of what is today the United States. By the time Andrew Jackson was an adult, many Americans were packing their belongings and heading west. When Europeans first came to North America, settlers had found the Appalachian Mountains difficult to cross. This rugged mountain range runs for hundreds of miles from New York south to Alabama and Georgia.

Later, hunters discovered the Cumberland Gap. The Gap is a low place where it is easy to travel across the Appalachians. Native Americans and animals had been using it for thousands of years. Once Americans found it, they began moving to Kentucky and lands beyond. Between 1775 and 1810, more than 200,000 settlers headed through the Gap to what was then the far West of the United States. Andrew Jackson, eager for adventure, would be among the first settlers to live on the frontier.

CHAPTER TWO

A NATION'S HERO

After his mother died, Andrew Jackson lived with relatives. He had a hard time getting along with them, however. So it was not very long before he was ready to leave the Waxhaws. By December of 1784, he had reached the age of 17. He was still tall and skinny, but he was also very strong. He was wild by nature. However, he had realized he wanted to do something important with his life. He moved to Salisbury, North Carolina, where he began to study law. Within two years, Andrew Jackson was a lawyer.

Jackson had always wanted to see the West. He was pleased when the North Carolina **legislature** hired him. The state sent him to its western frontier to work as a lawyer. North Carolina was much bigger than it is today. It stretched all the way to the Mississippi River. But soon its western part would become a new state, called Tennessee.

Jackson went from one frontier settlement to another, traveling on horseback to his destinations. In each new town, he argued a case in court. After a few years, he stopped traveling and settled in what was then a small town, Nashville. Jackson opened his own

Andrew Jackson married Rachel Donelson Robards in 1791. The couple loved each other deeply. They never had children of their own, but Rachel took in orphans and also helped raise her relatives' children. She and Andrew eventually adopted a son in 1809.

In Andrew Jackson's day, people did not become lawyers by going to law school. Instead, they studied with someone who was already a lawyer.

law office there and began to earn money. His clients often paid him with land instead of cash. Jackson also bought land as he earned more money.

In Nashville, Jackson lived in a boarding house owned by the Donelson family. In 1791, he married Mrs. Donelson's daughter Rachel. By this time, he was working as district attorney for several counties and also had his own law office. Soon, the territorial government appointed him the attorney general for the Southwest Territory or Mero District of North Carolina.

As a lawyer, Jackson learned a lot about government and the law. As time went by, he decided he wanted to become a politician. Then he would be involved in creating new laws for the country. In 1796, Tennessee became a state. Jackson became the first person from Tennessee elected to the House of Representatives. The next year, he was elected senator. But in 1798, he went back to Tennessee and became a judge. He also became an officer in the state militia.

By 1802, Jackson had been elected major general of the militia. He commanded many volunteer soldiers, training them to be prepared for Native American attacks. He soon became well known for

When Andrew Jackson arrived in Nashville, the town was nothing more than a few cabins, some tents made from bark, two taverns, two stores, and a courthouse built out of logs. A fence had been built around the village to keep out roaming buffalo.

Andrew Jackson was quick to take offense at what others said about him or his wife. He would challenge anyone who insulted him to a duel. Most of these challenges were settled quickly. Shots were fired in only one duel. Jackson killed his opponent and badly injured himself. This is an artist's portrayal of Jackson (on the right) during a duel.

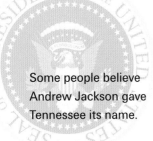

Some people believe Andrew Jackson gave Tennessee its name.

During the War of 1812, soldiers nicknamed Jackson "Old Hickory." They named him after this hard, rugged wood because he was so strong and tough.

his temper. When others made him angry, he would challenge them to duels, which are gunfights used to settle arguments.

In 1804, the Jacksons bought a new piece of land and turned it into a **plantation,** or large farm, where they grew such crops as cotton and corn. They called it The Hermitage. At first the Jacksons lived in a two-story log farmhouse. Later they hired workers to build a big, beautiful house. Jackson also had been buying slaves. He put them to work planting fields of cotton.

In 1806, Jackson retired from his position as a judge. He went into business operating a cotton gin and stores with some partners. He also devoted his attention to his plantation. Soon, however, he would work for his country as a military leader.

For many years, British ships had been stopping American ships at sea to keep the United States from trading its goods with other nations. American leaders demanded that the British government stop interfering with American trade, but it refused. In June 1812, the United States declared war on Great Britain. Jackson prepared the Tennessee militia to fight for the country. Jackson and his troops won many victories against Native Americans who were helping the British.

By April of 1814, the U.S. Army had made Jackson a general. A month later, he became commander of all American troops in Tennessee, Mississippi, and Louisiana. When British soldiers attacked Alabama, Jackson's men fought back and forced them to

This portrait of Andrew Jackson was painted when he was in his late forties. After working as a lawyer for many years, Jackson rejoined the army. He was such a good leader that he was made a general.

retreat. When the British fled to Florida, they were forced to retreat yet again.

In December of 1814, Jackson and his men went to New Orleans. Americans feared the British would soon attack that city. If they succeeded, they could block trade on the Mississippi River, leaving Americans short of supplies. The American soldiers went to help protect the city.

Soon after Jackson arrived, the British began to attack towns in southern Louisiana. On January 8, 1815, they attacked Jackson and his men. He beat them easily in the Battle of New Orleans.

Native Americans nicknamed Jackson "Sharpknife."

Andrew Jackson (on white horse) and his men easily won the Battle of New Orleans. It was an important victory for the United States, because it meant that a foreign power would never again control the Mississippi River Valley.

Americans rejoiced when they got the news of his victory. Actually, this battle had been fought after the war ended. In Europe, representatives of the United States and Great Britain had agreed to peace on December 24, 1814, but word had been slow to travel across the Atlantic Ocean.

Jackson was a national hero. He was known as a smart, courageous man and a great general, one who also had a bad temper at times. Few people knew that he was also devoted to his family and kind to his friends.

For a time, Jackson went home to his wife and son at The Hermitage. But new problems were brewing between U.S. citizens and the Native Americans of the South. At the time, Spain still controlled Florida. The Seminole were a Native American tribe that moved back and forth between Spanish Florida and American Georgia. They were angry because Americans were settling on their land. To scare them away, the Seminole raided American settlements. From camps in Florida, they rode across the border into Georgia. The tribe killed a few Americans and burned their property.

The American army announced it was going to stop the Native American raids. In 1818, Jackson put back on his uniform and took charge of the American

The Seminole still live in Florida, even though the U.S. government tried to drive them out.

Jackson's victory at the Battle of New Orleans made him a national hero. People were so proud of Jackson's victory that they hoped he would run for president one day.

soldiers in Georgia. After Native Americans killed some of his troops, Jackson was angry. He did not wait for government orders to tell him what to do. Instead, he and his men marched into Florida. They battled and beat the Seminole and captured Spanish forts.

Although some Americans thought Jackson should be punished for acting without orders, President James Monroe did not have him arrested. Jackson's actions ultimately helped the United States. Spain's leaders wanted to avoid more trouble, so they agreed to give all of Florida to the United States. Still, not every American leader was happy with Jackson. Some did not like the fact that he had taken such an enormous amount of power into his own hands.

RACHEL JACKSON

Andrew Jackson's wife, Rachel, was born in 1767 in Virginia. She came to Tennessee as a pioneer when she was 12. When she was 17, Rachel married her first husband, Lewis Robards. For some reason, Rachel and Robards separated and Rachel went to live with her mother. She met Andrew Jackson while he was living at her mother's boarding house. When Rachel and Andrew Jackson became friends, Robards said terrible things about her. Jackson wanted to protect Rachel.

In 1791, Rachel went to Natchez, Mississippi. While she was there, Robards began divorce proceedings. When Andrew Jackson asked her to marry him, she happily said yes. Jackson was a man well known for his temper, but Rachel was the love of his life. He treated her with great affection.

In 1793, Andrew and Rachel Jackson received bad news. They learned that Lewis Robards had never truly divorced her. A judge finally granted the divorce. Rachel and Andrew married a second time. Many years later, when Andrew Jackson ran for president, his political enemies wanted to make him look as bad as they could. They spread a rumor that Rachel had been married to two men at one time. Rachel had never truly wanted Jackson to become the president, and the campaign was very difficult for her. The rumor upset and embarrassed her so much that she became ill. Soon after Jackson won the election, Rachel had a heart attack and died. Until the end of his life, Jackson talked about how much he missed his wife and how much he hated those people who he blamed for her death.

C H A P T E R   T H R E E

HEADED FOR THE WHITE HOUSE

Andrew Jackson became a hero after he won the Battle of New Orleans, the last battle of the War of 1812. Many people thought he would one day become president. But this would not happen for more than 10 years.

In 1821, President Monroe asked Andrew Jackson to become the governor of Florida. The Jacksons moved to Pensacola, the Florida capital at that time. Jackson worked to build a new government. He divided the territory into counties and created a court system. But soon he quit his new job. He and Rachel went home to Tennessee. Some historians say this was because of disagreements Jackson had with President Monroe. Others say that Jackson quit because his health was poor.

Back at The Hermitage, Jackson's health improved. Early in 1822, Americans started to talk about who would run for president in 1824. Many people wanted Jackson to become a **candidate.** But first, he was reelected to the Senate. He returned to Washington,

The Jackson family traveled to Washington, D.C., in December 1824. They went there to find out who had been elected president. Many people expected it to be Jackson.

D.C. in 1823. When he was not working in the Senate, he was campaigning for the presidency.

Four men ran for president in 1824—John Quincy Adams, Henry Clay, William Crawford, and Andrew Jackson. Jackson received 43 percent of the vote—more than any of the other candidates. Still, he did not win the presidency. Although more Americans wanted Jackson than the other three candidates to be their new president, the **Electoral College** still had to cast their

As this political cartoon shows, the 1824 presidential election was a four-way race between (on the left) John Quincy Adams, William Crawford, Andrew Jackson, and (at right, scratching his head) Henry Clay.

votes. To win, Jackson had to receive more than half the electoral votes, and he did not.

According to the U.S. **Constitution,** the House of Representatives decides who will be president if a candidate does not receive a majority of the electoral votes. Henry Clay was Speaker of the House, the leader of the House of Representatives. He was very powerful, and he was able to convince other representatives how to vote. In public, Clay did not say whom he wanted to be president. But behind closed doors, he told other politicians that he thought Jackson would make a poor leader. Clay believed Jackson would not cooperate with Congress. He thought Jackson would

24

fight to achieve his own goals instead. Clay and John Quincy Adams met in secret. Clay agreed to help Adams win the House vote.

Thanks to Clay, John Quincy Adams won the election. Jackson and his supporters were outraged when Adams named Clay the secretary of state, one of the most important jobs in the president's **cabinet.** Jackson's

Jackson was furious that the House voted to make John Quincy Adams (left) president.

supporters said that Adams and his friends did not follow the wishes of the American people but did as they pleased.

Jackson returned to Tennessee after Adams's **inauguration.** He was already thinking about the next election. He promised himself that the next time, he would win no matter what. Many Americans still supported Jackson. Throughout the next four years, they criticized President Adams for the way Jackson had been treated.

During Adams's term, Jackson and his supporters created a new **political party,** the **Democrats.** Jackson was its unofficial leader. Jackson's supporters wrote newspaper articles explaining why people should vote for Democrats. They gave speeches to Americans,

Jackson attended a reception at the White House while John Quincy Adams was president. At the time, Jackson had already begun campaigning to win the next election.

26

promising to help those who had less money. In the past, American politicians often listened only to what wealthy Americans wanted from the government. Americans with less money, such as shopkeepers and farmers, liked the Democratic Party. They believed the Democrats were interested in helping them instead of the rich.

Jackson began to work for the presidency three years before the election of 1828. John Quincy Adams was still the president, but many people began to support Jackson. Jackson's supporters' efforts paid off, and he won the election in a landslide—a huge number of votes!

Although Jackson was pleased to be elected, it was a sad and difficult time for him. Just weeks after he won the election, on December 22, 1828, his wife Rachel died. Jackson traveled to Washington, D.C., alone.

In March of 1829, Jackson was sworn in at what became known as "the people's inaugural." He promised to turn the government over to the common man. To prove it, he opened the White House to ordinary Americans for the first time. Thousands of people swarmed into the elegant mansion. It was a mess! Some people accidentally broke things, while others spit tobacco juice on the carpet. People even stood on the chairs and sofas to get a good look at the mansion. Jackson didn't mind. He knew the people were acting this way because they were happy he had been elected.

In Washington, he set right to work getting his government set up. He decided to replace many

Jackson's niece, Emily Donelson, acted as the White House hostess when Jackson was president. All four of her children were born there.

27

Jackson easily won the 1828 presidential election. This illustration shows him greeting well-wishers while on his way to Washington, D.C., for his inauguration.

government employees. He fired nearly 1,000 of the 10,000 people who then worked for the government. Some of those he fired had been accused of stealing money from the government. He also took positions away from people who had held their jobs for many years. He believed new employees would help make government offices run better. He said they would work harder and bring new ideas to their jobs. Jackson filled most of these positions with his own supporters, who would be sure to help him accomplish his goals.

Newspapers reported that there were now government jobs available. Many people wrote or came to the White House, asking Jackson to hire them. Some of them were Democrats who had helped him get elected. Others were ordinary people looking for work as bookkeepers or secretaries. Jackson felt frustrated because he had to turn away many who wanted jobs.

Andrew Jackson subscribed to about 20 newspapers to keep up on political news.

Jackson, who considered himself a man of the people, invited the American public to his inauguration. Thousands of enthusiastic supporters crowded into the presidential mansion for the celebration, leaving the place a total mess.

CHAPTER FOUR

THE PRESIDENT'S POWER

As president, Andrew Jackson remained a fighter. He struggled hard to make the office of president very important. He also battled other politicians over very difficult issues.

When Jackson was elected president, a serious issue had already begun to divide the country, especially upsetting southerners. The government gave large amounts of money to northern and western states to build roads and canals. The South did not need these things, so it received less government money. Southerners thought this was unfair. So did Jackson, who believed the **federal** government should pay only for projects that helped all Americans. Congress passed a **bill** that gave Kentucky money for a new road. Kentucky was considered a western state at the time. Southerners complained

Although brokenhearted by the loss of his wife, Jackson entered the presidency determined to make big changes in the way government worked.

that others were still getting more than their fair share. Jackson refused to sign this bill. This pleased people in the South.

Southerners cheered Jackson yet again when he convinced Congress to pass the Indian Removal Act in 1830. This law said the president could order the army to move Native Americans off land that white Americans wanted. White settlers in Georgia and Alabama wanted the Creek, Cherokee, and Choctaw tribes to leave their states, even though they had lived there for centuries. In 1832, the Supreme Court, the most powerful court in the country, said that Native Americans had a right to the land on which they lived. Jackson ignored the court.

Jackson also did something that made him less popular in the South. His vice president, John C. Calhoun, was from South Carolina. Calhoun did not like a **tariff** that Congress had created in 1828. It meant that Americans had to pay a special tax on many materials that were brought to the United States from other countries, such as metals and fabrics. The tariff made the foreign items cost more, so that more people would buy American-made goods.

The southerners were against the tariff. They used more imported goods than other parts of the country, and they did not want to pay more for them. In addition, Great Britain bought cotton from the South to make into fabric and clothing. When Americans bought less of these things from Great Britain, the British bought less cotton from the South.

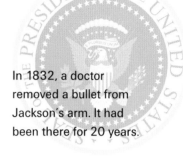

In 1832, a doctor removed a bullet from Jackson's arm. It had been there for 20 years.

THE TRAIL OF TEARS

Historians often call Andrew Jackson "the people's president" because he was interested in the problems of ordinary Americans. He wanted people who were not wealthy to have a voice in American government. Andrew Jackson did not believe in equality for all, however. He was a **racist** who believed that white people, because of the color of their skin, were better than blacks and Native Americans. He did not think people of other races deserved equal rights.

In fact, Andrew Jackson believed that white Americans had the right to take away land where Native Americans had lived for hundreds of years. He talked Congress into passing a law that gave the president the right to use the army to "remove" Native Americans from lands that white settlers wanted. This law would have far-reaching effects.

In 1836, militias in Georgia attacked the Creek, a Native American people. Creek homes were destroyed, and people began to starve. A few went to white settlements to steal food for their families. This upset white people. They called for the army to take the Creek away. Soldiers rounded them up and forced them to march west of the Mississippi.

In 1838, after Jackson left office as president, U.S. soldiers forced more than 16,000 Cherokee people from their homes east of the Mississippi River and ordered them to march westward to Oklahoma. As many as 4,000 of them died along the way. This tragic journey became known as the "Trail of Tears." Other tribes that were forcibly removed were the Chickasaw, the Choctaw, and the Seminole.

When Jackson became president, the White House still sat in the middle of farmland. He had a stone wall and wooden fence built to surround the house and its grounds.

Calhoun declared that his state would not pay the tariff. He believed that states had the right to nullify federal laws, which meant they could refuse to obey them. Jackson threatened to send troops to South Carolina to make its citizens obey the law. Calhoun finally backed down. Jackson then worked to lower the tariff. This matter left bad feelings between the North and South. Calhoun later stepped down as vice president and began to devote himself to helping the South. Eventually, the argument over states' rights would lead to the Civil War.

In 1832, the next presidential election was held. Jackson ran for reelection, and Martin Van Buren ran as his vice president. Many Americans still believed the Democrats were interested in helping ordinary people, so Jackson and Van Buren won easily.

Jackson had one major goal in his second term. He wanted to destroy the Second Bank of the United States, a private bank that held the government's money. He and his supporters thought the bank had grown too powerful. Jackson did not like the fact that

To Americans, President Jackson was still a great hero, and he was popular with the people. His strong will and determination to get his way often caused problems with other politicians, however.

a bank controlled by private businessmen had so much control over the country's economy without the government being able to have some say in the matter.

In 1832, Congress passed a law re-chartering—reauthorizing—the Bank. Jackson **vetoed** this bill. It was just one of many times he used the veto while president. By doing so, he made the office of president stronger, fighting Congress for power.

Jackson ordered that all the government's money be withdrawn from the Second Bank. The secretary of the **treasury** refused to obey his orders, so Jackson fired him. In September of 1833, the new secretary withdrew the money from the Second Bank.

The Senate was angry that Jackson had not asked it what to do. Its members decided Jackson had to be punished. They voted to censure him. When Congress censures the president, its members state formally that they believe he has done something wrong. Jackson replied by saying he did not have to do what the Senate wanted. He believed his responsibility was to the American people, not to other politicians. The Second Bank finally closed its doors, as Jackson had wanted.

In 1836, the next presidential election was held. At the time, there was no law that said a president could serve only two terms. Andrew Jackson could have run for president for a third time, but he was ill. He decided it was time for him to leave the White House. He was

GENERAL JACKSON SLAYING THE MANY HEADED MONSTER.

In 1816, the government gave the Second Bank of the United States the right to handle the country's money for the next 20 years. This meant the bank could print money whenever it wanted and make loans to whomever it wanted. It had great power over the country and its citizens. This cartoon shows President Jackson and Vice President Van Buren fighting a "many-headed monster" that symbolizes the bank.

Shortly before he died, Jackson posed for this photograph.

Andrew Jackson was the first president to ride a train while in office.

pleased when his vice president, Martin Van Buren, won the election. Jackson thought Van Buren would do a good job and continue the projects he had started. On March 4, 1837, Martin Van Buren was inaugurated as the eighth president of the United States. Jackson's political influence would remain for years.

Jackson went home to his beloved plantation in Tennessee. He had been away for a very long time, and The Hermitage needed a lot of work. He bought new farm equipment and made repairs to his house. He ordered his slaves to plant new crops. For a time, Jackson remained interested in politics. Politicians wrote to him, and he offered them advice.

But Jackson was growing weaker. By 1845, he was very sick. He had to spend most of his time in bed. Jackson realized that he would soon die.

On June 8, 1845, Andrew Jackson died at The Hermitage. He was 78 years old. Throughout his life, he fought hard to accomplish his goals. This fierce, stubborn man never let anyone stand in his way. As a general, he fought with all his might to protect the nation. As president, he wanted most of all to help Americans like himself, white people who were born without a fortune.

In turn, many of the nation's people admired him. In the end, what mattered most to Jackson was his country. "I thank God that my life has been spent in a land of liberty," Jackson once said, "and that He has given me a heart to love my country with the affection of a son."

THE HERMITAGE

When he was a young man, Andrew Jackson bought and sold many pieces of land in the area around Nashville. In 1804, he found a place so beautiful, he wanted to live there forever. He turned the land into a plantation and called it The Hermitage. Jackson chose this name because a hermit is someone who goes off into the wilderness to live alone. He wanted The Hermitage to be a place where he and his wife Rachel could escape the cares of the world and enjoy peace and quiet. They lived in a two-story log farmhouse at The Hermitage for the first 17 years. Then they began building a brick house, where they moved in 1821. In 1834, a few years after Rachel died, the brick house burned down. Jackson built a beautiful new mansion, which still stands today.

Over the years, Andrew Jackson bought and sold many slaves. They lived on The Hermitage plantation in small log and brick cabins. A few worked in Jackson's house, but most worked in his fields. They planted and tended huge fields of cotton and corn. They ran his cotton gin. They also took care of the plantation's livestock, especially the racehorses Jackson loved.

Andrew Jackson retired to The Hermitage when he left the presidency. He died there in 1845, and his son sold the plantation about 10 years later. Today it is open for visitors to tour and learn more about the nation's seventh president.

1760	1770	1780	1790	1800

1765
Andrew Jackson's parents come to America from Ireland.

1767
Andrew Jackson's father dies in March. Andrew is born just a few days later, on March 15.

1772
At age 5, Andrew Jackson has already learned to read. He starts to go to school.

1776
Andrew Jackson reads the Declaration of Independence to the people of his town.

1779
Hugh Jackson, the oldest of the Jackson boys, dies in battle.

1780
Local militia soldiers fight the British near the Jackson's home in what will become known as the Waxhaw Massacre. The Jackson family helps tend the wounded. After the battle, Andrew and his brother Robert join the American army.

1781
In April, the Jackson boys are captured by British soldiers and taken to prison. Their mother finally arranges for their release. Both boys are ill, and Robert dies as soon as they arrive home. Betty Jackson becomes ill and dies while nursing sick American prisoners of war. Andrew Jackson is the only surviving member of his family. He lives with relatives for the next three years.

1784
Jackson decides to study law.

1787
Jackson gets his law license and goes to western North Carolina to work as a lawyer. Eventually, he settles in Nashville, located in what will soon become the state of Tennessee. He opens his own law office.

1791
Jackson marries Rachel Donelson Robards.

1796
Jackson is elected to the U.S. House of Representatives.

1797
Jackson is elected to the U.S. Senate.

1798
Jackson becomes a judge in the state of Tennessee. He also becomes an officer in the Tennessee state militia.

1806
Jackson retires from his position as a judge and devotes his attention to The Hermitage, the plantation he and Rachel have built.

1809
Rachel and Andrew Jackson adopt a boy. They name him Andrew Jackson Jr.

1812

The United States declares war on Great Britain. The War of 1812 begins. Jackson joins the U.S. Army.

1814

The War of 1812 ends in December.

1815

Jackson becomes a national hero after he and his men beat the British in the Battle of New Orleans on January 8.

1818

Andrew Jackson leads American soldiers into Spanish Florida to fight the Seminole War. Jackson is made a general and then commander of all American troops in Tennessee, Mississippi, and Louisiana.

1821

President James Monroe appoints Jackson governor of the new territory of Florida. Jackson quits before the year is over.

1822

Some Americans begin to encourage Jackson to run for president in the next election, which will be held in 1824.

1823

Jackson is once again elected to the Senate.

1824

Jackson receives the most popular votes in the presidential election. He does not become president, however, because he has not won a majority of votes in the Electoral College. The House of Representatives votes for John Quincy Adams as president.

1825

Many Americans complain when Adams is sworn in as president. Jackson begins to campaign for the next election.

1828

Congress places tariffs on imported raw materials, angering many southerners. Jackson is elected president of the United States. His wife dies just weeks after his election.

1829

Almost immediately after he takes office, Jackson fires nearly 1,000 government employees. He gives many of the jobs to his supporters. Vice President Calhoun declares that the states can nullify federal laws believed to be unconstitutional.

1830

Jackson convinces Congress to pass the Indian Removal Act.

1832

Jackson ignores a Supreme Court ruling stating that Native Americans in Georgia have a right to keep their land. He issues the Nullification Proclamation. Jackson is elected to a second term. His new vice president is Martin Van Buren. Jackson begins his fight to destroy the Second Bank of the United States, which he feels has become too powerful.

1833

All government money is withdrawn from the Second Bank of the United States. It is later forced to close.

1834

The Senate censures Jackson because it believes he had no right to remove money from the Second Bank without approval from Congress.

1836

Jackson refuses to run for president for a third term. His vice president, Martin Van Buren, is elected the eighth president of the United States.

1837

After Van Buren's inauguration, Jackson returns home to Tennessee.

1845

Andrew Jackson dies on June 8.

GLOSSARY

bill (BILL) A bill is an idea for a new law that is presented to a group of lawmakers. When Congress passed a bill to pay for new roads in Kentucky, Jackson refused to sign it.

cabinet (KAB-ih-net) A cabinet is the group of people who advise a president. The secretary of state is part of the president's cabinet.

campaign (kam-PAYN) A campaign is the process of running for an election, including activities such as giving speeches or attending rallies. Jackson's first campaign was difficult for his wife.

candidate (KAN-dih-det) A candidate is a person running in an election. Americans wanted Jackson to be a presidential candidate in the 1824 election.

cavalry (KAV-uhl-ree) Cavalry are soldiers who fight on horseback. During the Revolutionary War, Andrew Jackson and his brother were assigned to the cavalry.

cholera (KOL-ur-uh) Cholera is a dangerous disease that causes severe illness and diarrhea. Andrew Jackson's mother died of cholera.

colonies (KOL-uh-neez) The Colonies were the American areas ruled by Great Britain before 1775. The colonies became the first 13 states of the United States.

constitution (kon-stih-TOO-shun) A constitution is the set of basic principles that govern a state, country, or society. The U.S. Constitution says the House of Representatives decides who will be president when no candidate wins a majority of electoral votes.

Democrats (DEM-uh-kratz) Democrats are members of the Democratic political party, one of the two major political parties in the United States. Jackson and his friends formed the Democratic Party.

Electoral College (ee-LEKT-uh-rul KAWL-ij) The Electoral College is made up of representatives from each state who vote for candidates in presidential elections. Members of the Electoral College cast their votes according to the candidate that most people in their state prefer.

federal (FED-er-ul) Federal means having to do with the central government of the United States, rather than a state or city government. John Calhoun believed that states had the right to ignore federal laws.

frontier (frun-TEER) A frontier is a region that is at the edge of or beyond settled land. As a young man, Jackson went to the western frontier to work as a lawyer.

immigrants (IM-uh-grunts) Immigrants are people who come from one country to live in another country. Jackson's parents were immigrants from Ireland.

inauguration (ih-nawg-yuh-RAY-shun) An inauguration is the ceremony that takes place when a new president begins a term. Jackson's inauguration was known as "the people's inauguration."

legislature (LEJ-ih-slay-chur) A legislature is the part of a government that makes laws. The North Carolina legislature sent Jackson to the West as a lawyer.

militias (muh-LISH-uhz) Militias are volunteer armies, made up of citizens who have trained as soldiers. During the Revolution, militias were formed to fight the British.

patriots (PAY-tree-uts) A patriot was any of the American colonists who wanted independence from Britain. As a young man, many of Jackson's friends and neighbors were patriots.

plantation (plan-TAY-shun) A plantation is a large farm found in warm climates where crops are grown. Andrew Jackson and his wife owned a plantation in Tennessee called The Hermitage.

political party (puh-LIT-ih-kul PAR-tee) A political party is a group of people who share similar ideas about how to run a government. Jackson helped form the Democratic political party.

racist (RAY-sist) A racist is a person who thinks his or her race is superior to others. Jackson was a racist because he believed white people were better than blacks and Native Americans.

retreat (ree-TREET) If an army retreats, it moves back or withdraws to avoid danger or defeat. Jackson's men forced the British to retreat in several battles during the War of 1812.

revolution (rev-uh-LOO-shun) A revolution is something that causes a complete change in government. The American Revolution was a war fought between the United States and Great Britain from 1775 to 1783.

smallpox (SMAWL-poks) Smallpox is a very contagious disease that causes chills, fever, and pimples that leave scars. Andrew and his brother became sick with smallpox while in a British prison camp during the Revolutionary War.

tariff (TAYR-iff) A tariff is a tax on foreign goods. Southerners in the 1800s used many foreign goods, so they did not want tariffs on them.

treasury (TREZH-ur-ee) A treasury manages a government's money, including its income and expenses. The secretary of the treasury is in charge of the government's money.

veto (VEE-toh) The veto is the right of the president to reject a bill that has been passed by Congress and to keep it from becoming a law. Andrew Jackson vetoed many bills while president.

THE UNITED STATES GOVERNMENT

The United States government is divided into three equal branches: the executive, the legislative, and the judicial. This division helps prevent abuses of power because each branch has to answer to the other two. No one branch can become too powerful.

EXECUTIVE BRANCH

PRESIDENT
VICE PRESIDENT
DEPARTMENTS

The job of the executive branch is to enforce the laws. It is headed by the president, who serves as the spokesperson for the United States around the world. The president signs bills into law and appoints important officials such as federal judges. He or she is also the commander in chief of the U.S. military. The president is assisted by the vice president, who takes over if the president dies or cannot carry out the duties of the office.

The executive branch also includes various departments, each focused on a specific topic. They include the Defense Department, the Justice Department, and the Agriculture Department. The department heads, along with other officials such as the vice president, serve as the president's closest advisers, called the cabinet.

LEGISLATIVE BRANCH

CONGRESS
Senate and
House of Representatives

The job of the legislative branch is to make the laws. It consists of Congress, which is divided into two parts: the Senate and the House of Representatives. The Senate has 100 members, and the House of Representatives has 435 members. Each state has two senators. The number of representatives a state has varies depending on the state's population.

Besides making laws, Congress also passes budgets and enacts taxes. In addition, it is responsible for declaring war, maintaining the military, and regulating trade with other countries.

JUDICIAL BRANCH

SUPREME COURT
COURTS OF APPEALS
DISTRICT COURTS

The job of the judicial branch is to interpret the laws. It consists of the nation's federal courts. Trials are held in district courts. During trials, judges must decide what laws mean and how they apply. Courts of appeals review the decisions made in district courts.

The nation's highest court is the Supreme Court. If someone disagrees with a court of appeals ruling, he or she can ask the Supreme Court to review it. The Supreme Court may refuse. The Supreme Court makes sure that decisions and laws do not violate the Constitution.

CHOOSING THE PRESIDENT

It may seem odd, but American voters don't elect the president directly. Instead, the president is chosen using what is called the Electoral College.

Each state gets as many votes in the Electoral College as its combined total of senators and representatives in Congress. For example, Iowa has two senators and five representatives, so it gets seven electoral votes. Although the District of Columbia does not have any voting members in Congress, it gets three electoral votes. Usually, the candidate who wins the most votes in any given state receives all of that state's electoral votes.

To become president, a candidate must get more than half of the Electoral College votes. There are a total of 538 votes in the Electoral College, so a candidate needs 270 votes to win. If nobody receives 270 Electoral College votes, the House of Representatives chooses the president.

With the Electoral College system, the person who receives the most votes nationwide does not always receive the most electoral votes. This happened most recently in 2000, when Al Gore received half a million more national votes than George W. Bush. Bush became president because he had more Electoral College votes.

THE WHITE HOUSE

The White House is the official home of the president of the United States. It is located at 1600 Pennsylvania Avenue NW in Washington, D.C. In 1792, a contest was held to select the architect who would design the president's home. James Hoban won. Construction took eight years.

The first president, George Washington, never lived in the White House. The second president, John Adams, moved into the house in 1800, though the inside was not yet complete. During the War of 1812, British soldiers burned down much of the White House. It was rebuilt several years later.

The White House was changed through the years. Porches were added, and President Theodore Roosevelt added the West Wing. President William Taft changed the shape of the presidential office, making it into the famous Oval Office. While Harry Truman was president, the old house was discovered to be structurally weak. All the walls were reinforced with steel, and the rooms were rebuilt.

Today, the White House has 132 rooms (including 35 bathrooms), 28 fireplaces, and 3 elevators. It takes 570 gallons of paint to cover the outside of the six-story building. The White House provides the president with many ways to relax. It includes a putting green, a jogging track, a swimming pool, a tennis court, and beautifully landscaped gardens. The White House also has a movie theater, a billiard room, and a one-lane bowling alley.

PRESIDENTIAL PERKS

The job of president of the United States is challenging. It is probably one of the most stressful jobs in the world. Because of this, presidents are paid well, though not nearly as well as the leaders of large corporations. In 2007, the president earned $400,000 a year. Presidents also receive extra benefits that make the demanding job a little more appealing.

★ **Camp David:** In the 1940s, President Franklin D. Roosevelt chose this heavily wooded spot in the mountains of Maryland to be the presidential retreat, where presidents can relax. Even though it is a retreat, world business is conducted there. Most famously, President Jimmy Carter met with Middle Eastern leaders at Camp David in 1978. The result was a peace agreement between Israel and Egypt.

★ *Air Force One:* The president flies on a jet called *Air Force One.* It is a Boeing 747-200B that has been modified to meet the president's needs.

Air Force One is the size of a large home. It is equipped with a dining room, sleeping quarters, a conference room, and office space. It also has two kitchens that can provide food for up to 50 people.

★ **The Secret Service:** While not the most glamorous of the president's perks, the Secret Service is one of the most important. The Secret Service is a group of highly trained agents who protect the president and the president's family.

★ **The Presidential State Car:** The presidential limousine is a stretch Cadillac DTS.

It has been armored to protect the president in case of attack. Inside the plush car are a foldaway desk, an entertainment center, and a communications console.

★ **The Food:** The White House has five chefs who will make any food the president wants. The White House also has an extensive wine collection.

★ **Retirement:** A former president receives a pension, or retirement pay, of just under $180,000 a year. Former presidents also receive Secret Service protection for the rest of their lives.

FACTS

QUALIFICATIONS

To run for president, a candidate must

- ★ be at least 35 years old
- ★ be a citizen who was born in the United States
- ★ have lived in the United States for 14 years

TERM OF OFFICE

A president's term of office is four years.
No president can stay in office for more than two terms.

ELECTION DATE

The presidential election takes place every four years on the first Tuesday of November.

INAUGURATION DATE

Presidents are inaugurated on January 20.

OATH OF OFFICE

I do solemnly swear I will faithfully execute the office of the President of the United States and will to the best of my ability preserve, protect, and defend the Constitution of the United States.

WRITE A LETTER TO THE PRESIDENT

One of the best things about being a U.S. citizen is that Americans get to participate in their government. They can speak out if they feel government leaders aren't doing their jobs. They can also praise leaders who are going the extra mile. Do you have something you'd like the president to do? Should the president worry more about the environment and encourage people to recycle? Should the government spend more money on our schools? You can write a letter to the president to say how you feel!

1600 Pennsylvania Avenue
Washington, D.C. 20500
You can even send an e-mail to: president@whitehouse.gov

BOOKS

Behrman, Carol H. *Andrew Jackson.* Minneapolis: Lerner Publications, 2005.

Bruchac, Joseph. *Trail of Tears.* New York: Random House, 1999.

Feinberg, Barbara Silberdick. *America's First Ladies.* New York: Franklin Watts, 1998.

Ferry Steven. *Martin Van Buren.* Mankato, MN: The Child's World, 2009.

Stanley, George. *Andrew Jackson: Young Patriot.* New York: Aladdin Books, 2003.

VIDEOS

The American President. DVD, VHS (Alexandria, VA: PBS Home Video, 2000).

The History Channel Presents The Presidents. DVD (New York: A & E Home Video, 2005).

The History Channel Presents The War of 1812. DVD (New York: A & E Home Video, 2004).

National Geographic's Inside the White House. DVD (Washington, D.C.: National Geographic Video, 2003).

Rachel and Andrew Jackson. DVD, VHS (Alexandria, VA: PBS Home Video, 2006).

INTERNET SITES

Visit our Web page for lots of links about Andrew Jackson and other U.S. presidents:

http://www.childsworld.com/links

Note to Parents, Teachers, and Librarians: We routinely verify our Web links to make sure they are safe, active sites—so encourage your readers to check them out!